Note to Parents and Teachers

The READING ABOUT: STARTERS series introduces key science vocabulary and concepts to young children while encouraging them to discover and understand the world around them. The series works as a set of graded readers in three levels.

LEVEL 3: READ ALONE follows guidelines set out in the National Curriculum for Year 3 in schools. These books can be read alone or as part of guided or group reading. Each book has three sections:

• Information pages that introduce key concepts. Key words appear in bold for easy recognition on pages where the related science concepts are explained.
• A lively story that recalls this vocabulary and encourages children to use these words when they talk and write.
• A quiz asks children to look back and recall what they have read.

WHERE WILDLIFE LIVES looks at HABITATS. Below are some answers and activities related to the questions on the information spreads that parents, carers and teachers can use to discuss and develop further ideas and concepts:

p. 6 *Where would you find a woodlouse, worm, snail, butterfly or frog?* Woodlice are found under logs, worms in the soil, snails in damp places, butterflies near flowers and frogs in a pond.

p. 9 *Can you think of any other predators and the prey that they eat?* Ask children to think about predators and prey in different habitats, e.g. shark and fish in the sea, blackbird and worm in garden, or polar bear and seal in the Arctic.

p. 11 *What other animals have adapted to life in towns?* e.g. squirrels and pigeons. Ask children how animals have adapted to life in other habitats, e.g. deserts or the Arctic.

p. 13 *What other sounds might you hear in a wood or forest?* e.g. birdsong, rustling in leaves. Ask about sounds you might hear in other habitats, e.g. seashore, river, meadow.

p. 15 *Why should they be careful not to touch insects?* Some insects can give a painful sting or bite. You could also warn children about other animals that sting or bite, e.g. jellyfish, crabs, spiders, prickly sea urchins, as well as stinging plants such as nettles.

p. 17 *What might she find (in pond or river water)?* Insects such as whirligigs and water boatmen, water snails, mosquito larvae, frogspawn and water plants.

p. 19 *When is a good time to look for seashells?* When the tide is out.

p. 21 *What other animals can you spot inside your home?* Look out for flying insects such as flies and wasps, creepy crawlies such as ants and birds nesting in the roof.

ADVISORY TEAM

Educational Consultant
Andrea Bright – Science Co-ordinator, Trafalgar Junior School, Twickenham

Literacy Consultant
Jackie Holderness – former Senior Lecturer in Primary Education, Westminster Institute, Oxford Brookes University

Series Consultants
Anne Fussell – Early Years Teacher and University Tutor, Westminster Institute, Oxford Brookes University

David Fussell – C.Chem., FRSC

CONTENTS

© Aladdin Books Ltd 2005

Designed and produced by
Aladdin Books Ltd
2/3 Fitzroy Mews
London W1T 6DF

First published in
Great Britain in 2005 by
Franklin Watts
96 Leonard Street
London EC2A 4XD

A catalogue record for this
book is available from the
British Library.

ISBN 0 7496 6270 0 (H'bk)

ISBN 0 7496 6385 5 (P'bk)

Editor: Sally Hewitt
Design: Flick, Book Design
and Graphics

Thanks to:
• Ciannait O'Donnell, Georgia
Jedwab and Hugh and Luke
Pullman, for appearing as models
in this book.
• Ronan O'Donnell and Rob
Pullman for helping to organise
the photoshoots.
• The pupils and teachers of
Trafalgar Junior School,
Twickenham and St. Nicholas
C.E. Infant School, Wallingford,
for testing the sample books.

Photocredits:
l-left, r-right, b-bottom, t-top,
c-centre, m-middle
Cover tl, 17br — Ronan O'Donnell.
Cover rr, 11br, 16m, 20tr, 21t,
29br — Flick Smith. Cover tm —
Otto Rogge Photography. Cover
main — Comstock. 4tl, 21br, 31bl
— Digital Vision. 4b, 5t, 6mc, 8b,
9tc, 13bl, 31tr, 31ml, 31brc —
Corbis. 5m, 15tr, 23t, 31mr —
TongRo. 5b — Marc Arundale/
Select Pictures. 6br, 7 both, 9tr, 24br,
28bl — Stockbyte. 8tl, 11mr, 13tl,
25tl, 30mr — John Foxx Images.
9tl, 21bl, 23br — USDA. 9bl —
US Fish & Wildlife. 9br, 26br —
Ingram Publishing. 10tr, 24l, 25br,
26tr & ml, 27br, 28-29m both —
Jim Pipe. 10b, 11ml, 14br, 16br,
22tr, 24tr — Digital Vision. 12b,
16m, 20b — US Fish & Wildlife.
13mr, 19t — Corel. 18l — EU
archive. 21ml & bl — Photodisc.

READING ABOUT

Starters

HABITATS

Where Wildlife Lives

by Jim Pipe

Aladdin/Watts

London • Sydney

HABITATS

A home is a place where we can eat, drink, sleep, work and play.

Animals and plants need homes too. They need a place where there is food, water, shelter and space to live in.

This place is called a **habitat**.

Mountain habitat

Habitats can be big or small. They can be wet or dry, hot or cold, bright or dark.

Some habitats are huge areas like deserts, mountains or the sea.

Local habitats are woods, ponds, rivers, meadows and the seashore.

Small places like a patch of grass or a windowbox are habitats too.

LIVING THINGS

All **living things** need a habitat to live in.

Plants and animals usually share a habitat with other **living things**.

Look at this woodland scene. What **living things** can you spot?

Wood

Not all living things are plants or animals.

Mushrooms are living things called fungi.

Butterfly in the air

Where would you expect to find a woodlouse, worm, snail, butterfly or frog?

All sorts of **living things** share the same habitat. They use the habitat in different ways.

In a river, some plants grow underwater. Trees and bushes live on the river bank.

Fish live underwater, but birds and insects live on it.

Deer and mice live on land near the river.

Birds on the water

Fish underwater

FOOD CHAINS

A habitat provides living things with food and water.

Plants make food from sunlight and from minerals in the soil. Plants are food for many animals from caterpillars to elephants!

Zebras eat grass

Lions eat zebras

Plant-eating animals are often eaten by other animals, called predators.
The animals that predators eat are their prey.

Aphids eat plants → **Ladybirds eat aphids** → **Starlings eat ladybirds**

A **food chain** shows what living things eat in a habitat. The arrows go from one living thing to the living thing that eats it.

Can you draw a **food chain** showing that zebras eat grass and lions eat zebras?

Rabbit

Fox

Look at this pair of animals. The fox is the predator and the rabbit is its prey.

Can you think of any other predators and the prey that they eat?

EXPLORING HABITATS

We share habitats with other animals and plants.
If you want to **explore** a habitat, remember that is their home too.

Try to watch animals without disturbing them. If you touch pond water or soil, remember to wash your hands afterwards.

If you move an animal, return it to the place where you found it.

Take care near water

Always take a grown-up when you go **exploring**.

Most kinds of plant and animal have lived in the same habitat for thousands of years. Their body suits the habitat they live in.

If we damage a habitat, the animals in it may not be able to live anywhere else.

This dolphin can't live in a forest.

This gibbon can't live in the sea.

Some kestrels hunt in towns and cities. They have changed, or adapted, to a new habitat.

Kestrel

What other animals have adapted to life in towns?

TREES AND WOODS

One **tree** can be a habitat for thousands of living things.

Centipedes hunt slugs and worms in the rotting leaves at the base of a **tree**.

Weevils and beetles feed on **tree** bark. Bugs and caterpillars nibble new leaves.

Weevil

Tree

Trees grow together to form **woods** and forests, a habitat for all sorts of animals.

Birds and squirrels make their nests in **trees**.
They eat nuts, berries and the minibeasts that live on **trees**.

Squirrel　　**Deer**

Larger animals such as deer and badgers live on the forest floor.

Woodpecker

Forest animals are hard to spot. But you can listen for the noises they make. Woodpeckers looking for insects tap on tree trunks.

What other sounds might you hear in a wood or forest?

MEADOWS

When a field is left uncut it grows into a **meadow** of tall grasses and wild flowers.

Many flowers live in a **meadow**, such as thistles, buttercups, poppies and foxgloves.

Their bright colours attract insects such as bees, wasps and butterflies.

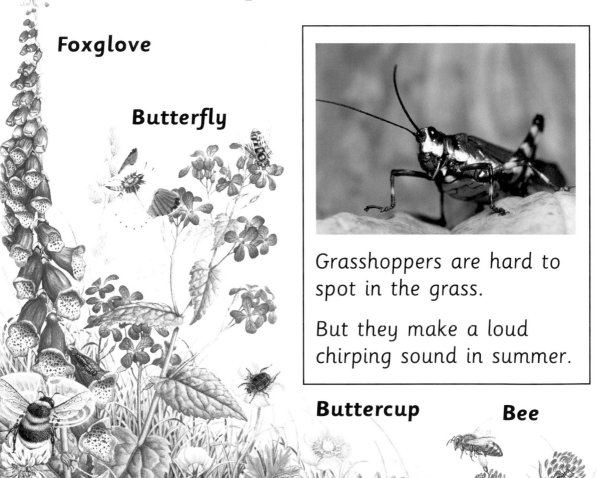

Foxglove

Butterfly

Grasshoppers are hard to spot in the grass.

But they make a loud chirping sound in summer.

Buttercup

Bee

These children are catching insects in a net.

Why should they be careful not to touch the insects?

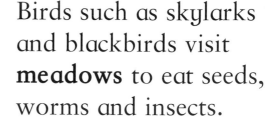

Birds such as skylarks and blackbirds visit **meadows** to eat seeds, worms and insects.

Mammals such as mice and rabbits make their homes in holes underground.

Foxes and owls hunt them at night.

Blackbird

Blackberries

Thistles

PONDS AND RIVERS

Many animals live in and around **ponds** and **rivers**. Insects, turtles and fish feed on plants that live underwater.

Dragonfly

Insects such as whirligigs and pond skaters live on the surface of the water.

Dragonflies and frogs hunt flies that live in the air above a **pond**.

Frog

Whirligig

16

Unlike a **pond**, the water in a **river** is always moving.

Kingfisher

Ducks and swans live on the water. They eat plants and insects. They build nests on the **river** bank.

Kingfishers and otters live on **river** banks. They hunt for fish under the water.

Otters

This girl is pond dipping. She uses a jar to collect water from a river.

She uses a magnifying glass to spot small animals in the water. What might she find?

THE SEASHORE

The **seashore** is home to many unusual plants and animals.

On a sandy beach, clams and other shellfish bury themselves in the sand.

Clam

Beach

Crabs scuttle across the beach, using their large claws to grab prey.

Higher up the beach, long grasses live in the sand dunes.

Seaweed

Starfish

The sea moves up and down the beach twice a day. This is called the tide.

When is a good time to look for seashells?

On a rocky beach, pools are left behind when the tide goes out. Plants called seaweed cling to rocks.

Limpets feed on the seaweed and in turn are prey for starfish. Small fish and crabs hunt prawns hiding in the seaweed.

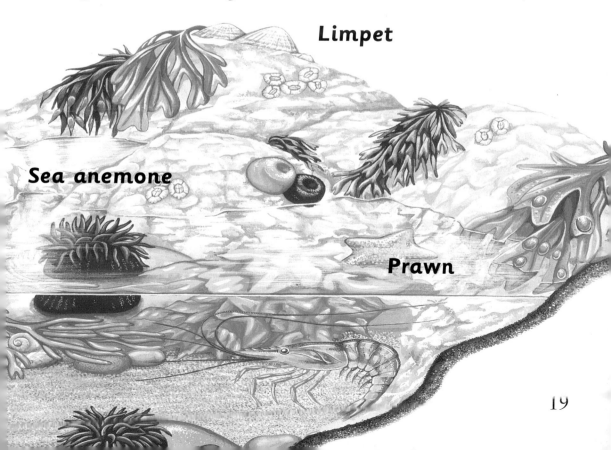

Limpet

Sea anemone

Prawn

TOWN WILDLIFE

Many animals have learned to live in a **town** or city habitat.

The trees and bushes in parks provide food and shelter for insects, birds, squirrels and even deer.

At night, foxes hunt for food in city dustbins.

We can help town wildlife by leaving out food.

We can plant flowers that attract insects.

Town pond

Town houses are a habitat for all sorts of birds. Pigeons nest on high buildings. Sparrows nest under roofs.

Mice and rats can live inside walls or under floors.

Minibeasts such as moths, cockroaches, ants and beetles can live inside your house.

Some animals help to keep our home clean. Spiders eat flies which spread germs.

What other animals can you spot inside your home?

Spider

Some animals live on us, such as fleas, nits and ticks!

Tick

HABITATS IN DANGER

Some habitats are in **danger**. When people cut down forests or turn meadows into farms, they kill wild plants.

They also destroy animal homes. Some animals die straight away. Others try to move to a new home.

The new home may not have enough food and shelter for extra animals.

Cutting down trees

We also damage habitats and wildlife when we pollute them with oil or chemicals.

Pollution

22

Meadow

We can also create new habitats.
We can let an area of grass
grow long to create a meadow.

We can plant a tree. One day it will be a
home to lots of animals. We can build a
pond to make a home for water creatures.

Digging a pond

Look around your
school or home.
How could you make
new habitats for
animals to live in?

SEASIDE EXPLORERS

*Look out for words and ideas
about habitats and living things.*

It was a lovely spring day.
Dan and James were feeling
bored in the house, so Dad took them to the beach.

"It's a bit cold to go
swimming," said Dan.
"Yes, but look at all that
sand," said James.
"Let's go exploring!"

"A beach is a home for lots
of living things," said Dad.
"Let's see how many we
can find."

"There are lots of different
places to look," said Dan.
"On the way here I saw
seagulls on the cliffs."

"I hope we see dolphins," said James.
"Let's climb up to the sand dunes.
We can see far out to sea from there."

"I can see some animals,"
said Dan.
"That family is having a
picnic in the long grass!"

"Do you think they're wild?" joked James.

The boys looked for rabbits in the dunes.
"They may be hiding underground in their burrows,"
said Dad. "Lots of predators like to eat rabbits!"

"I've found a paw print!"
shouted James.

"It looks like a dog's
paw," said Dan.
"I saw a woman walking
her dog along the beach!"

The boys walked
towards the sea.
Below the dunes was a
line of seaweed and shells.
"Look how far the tide
comes in," said Dan.

"What's this long shell?" asked James.
"It's a razor-shell," said Dad. "It's the shell from
an animal that burrows into the sand."

Further along the beach,
Dan found a starfish.
"I hope the tide comes in soon
and washes it back to sea."

The boys explored
the beach for two more hours. But
they found only shells and seaweed.

"Don't worry," said Dad. "I know a
rocky beach we can go to tomorrow."

The next day, Dan spotted some familiar faces
when they arrived at the rocky beach.
"It's that family from the sand dunes."

"The girl is collecting shells
on the beach," said Dad.
"Maybe she knows a good
place to look for animals."

Paula lived near the
beach and knew it well.
She showed the boys
some different types
of seaweed.

Then they walked over
to the rockpools.
"Watch out,"
said Paula.
"These rocks are
very slippery."

All around the rockpool, limpets
and periwinkles clung to the rocks.

"Some people scrape limpets off
the rocks," said Paula.
"But they're food for many
crabs and starfish."

Paula pointed out some
sea anemones.
"They look pretty, but they
are deadly predators,"
she said.
"They attack prey with
their poison tentacles."

"There's a little
fish in the rocks. Will the
anemone get it?" asked Dan.

"Phew! It got away this time."

Something else was moving under the water. It was a hermit crab.

"You can pick it up if you are gentle," said Dad. "Watch out, even tiny claws can pinch!"

When he had shown the boys, Dad put the crab back where he found it. It scuttled under a big stone.

As they walked back along the beach, the children were attacked by a big swarm of flies.

"The flies lay their eggs in the seaweed," said Paula. "But they love to suck blood from bigger animals like us. Run for it!"

"Thanks for showing us the rockpools," said Dan.
"You never know what you'll find," said Paula.
"The seashore is a habitat for so many animals."

Suddenly, James shouted out, "Look! It's a seal!"

"Is that his home?" asked Dan.
"Sort of," said Paula.
"His home stretches all around the world – it's the sea!"

WRITE YOUR OWN STORY about exploring a habitat. You also could do a drawing of a habitat showing where different animals and plants live, like this picture of a beach.

Seagulls

Rabbits

Crabs

Seaweed

Razor-shells

Fish

Limpets

Starfish

Seals

QUIZ

Are all living things plants or animals?

Answer on pages 6

What does a lion eat?

Is a lion a predator or prey?

Answer on page 8

How can we create new habitats?

Answer on page 23

What habitats are a home for these living things?

Weevil   Kingfisher

Clam

Dolphin

Answers on pages 12, 17, 18, 25

INDEX